MY KIND OF ANIMAL

MY KIND OF ANIMAL

Poems by Jefferson Carter

chax press : tucson : 2010

Acknowledgments:

Grateful acknowledgment is made to the following publications in
which some of these poems first appeared, often in slightly different
versions.

Birmingham Poetry Review, "Measuring"
Cutthroat, "Anarchists," "Helen," "The Oral Tradition"
Restoring Connections: the Sky Island Alliance Newsletter, "Grid"
Sandscript, "Abu Ghraib (A True Story)," "Like"
10X3 Plus, "The Nature of Beauty," "Please"

ISBN 978 0925904 83 6

Published by Chax Press
411 N 7th Ave Ste 103
Tucson, Arizona 85705-8388
USA

for Connie and for Evan

. . . siempre

CONTENTS

PLEASE

I wake up,
eye-to-eye with the cat's anus.
He's purring on my chest.
Why me, oh, Lord?
Like face time
with a rusty washer.
I hear good things
about the ungulates,
their table manners, their
clean plates. My kind
of animal, sweet-smelling,
modest, not like cats
weaving between your legs,
scent glands under their tails,
rubbing until you smell
like them, safe enough
to love. Take my species,
for example. I'm a person,
p-e-r-s-o-n. Before
the plague of white-eyes,
each nation called itself
"the people." Take
my species. Please.

THE ORAL TRADITION

for Steve

Sometimes, in conversation,
he'll look away & say
I don't want to talk about it.
I respect that. I really do
but like some nosey Homeric hero
I can feel the words piling up
behind my teeth's barrier:
tell me, godammit! Tell me
everything so we can be friends!
I like to imagine the real
oral tradition, those epic heroes
all sitting around the cook fires,
gossiping, trading recipes, even
consoling one another as they
mend the horsehair plumes,
the helmets heavy in their laps.

GOODBYE, ROTANDO

Cacking clastanets, I mean,
clacking castanets. You promised

we'd amble arm-in-arm
through the rotting suburbs.

Salt for thought, this
chipping silver off the backs

of mirrors, our struggle
against appearances.

When I said "Get
out of town," I didn't mean

"Get out of town."
It's an expression, like

"No way!" or "You shittin' me?"
or "Wish you were here."

GRID

I can tell by your outfit
that you are a cowboy.
Not a tourist. Not a hipster
or a roadie. Like you,
I was someone else.
Then I saw the singer
reading the lyrics & I knew
she was faking her orgasm.
Easting 530,550 meters,
northing 2,622,660 meters,
welcome to this high
Sonoran plant community,
this grid of wildcat roads
like exploded chromosomes.
No red arrow marking
your location? Believe me:
you are here.

DON'T GET ME STARTED

Last night at yoga
I listened to Elliot breathing
next to me like a patient
on a respirator. What if
there really is a soul?
Something the color
of duct tape or transparent
as plastic sheeting?
"Think about it," I say
at breakfast. My wife glares
& tries to hide behind the classifieds.
She's tired of my negative bullshit.
"Duct tape! Plastic sheeting!
Gee, I wonder why they're
pushing petroleum products?"
She leaves the table, her toast
untouched. Remember
chanting One! Two!
Three! Four! we don't
want your fucking war?
Remember that poster, girls say
yes to boys who say no?
I said to a girl across the room

what if they gave a war
& nobody came? I meant it,
it wasn't bullshit, but she untied
her macrame halter top anyway.
I like that slogan, no blood
for oil. Maybe I'll record it
on our answering machine or
shout it from our porch.
"You know," calls my wife
from the other room, "if you were
happier, you'd be happier."

ABU GHRAIB (A TRUE STORY)

After 24 hours
nonstop rap, you
could hear them
in their cells,
calling "Whazzup,
whazzup, whazzup?"

                We
finally got it right.
Top 40 country,
one hour & they're
howling "Mister!
Mister, please! No more!"

                The blues, then,
for the ones we broke,
Arabic versions of "Help
the poor. Baby,
help poor me."

STEAM

I don't think Blake meant
you must create your own

style or be enslaved by another's.
I don't know emo from baby ho.

I do know corpse pose, how
to visualize myself as a body

of water. It's raining, the surface
of the lake steaming. I know

the true story of Jesse Owens.
Jesse, Jesse, he's our man!!

Nigger, you can't sleep here.

16

ANARCHISTS

They blackballed me because I talk
too much & wear a pink fanny pack.
What? An anarchist can't be
in touch with his softer side?
We charged the Border Patrol outpost,
dodging bullets, little puffs of sand
spraying our ankles as we dived
for cover among the cholla. No one
complained then about my peppy
chatter or my fanny pack stuffed
with blasting caps. To make a long story
short, my first shipment of L. Ron Hubbard
epics arrived today. Tom Cruise would
never say you throw bombs like a girl.

BOSS TOOTH

Whitman wrote "the boss-tooth
advances in darkness." What
a kidder. Exhausted or primitive,
each culture buries its very own
toothed sex organ. Just ask
those teens driving by, bouncing
around in the car like wet puppies.
The boss tooth commands the little
teeth, everyone knows that, even
some Confederate amputee
coughing & sweating on his cot.

HOTLINE

*Common in plastics, phthalates and other
endocrine disruptors 'feminize' male anatomy.*
—Arizona Daily Star

Your male fish laying eggs?
Your anogenital distance shrinking?
I measure the distance
between my testicles & my anus
& call the Endocrine Disruption Hotline.
What's the normal male anogenital distance?
Twice the female anogenital distance
answers the recorded voice.
My wife wears nothing but sweat socks
& my old football jersey in bed.
She's snoring. I put on my reading glasses
& reach under my pillow for the ruler.

EXEMPT

Of course, traffic laws
don't apply to you. City buses
& narcissists exempt. Self-love
isn't the problem. You read
the sign "Pedestrian Improvement
Project" & think, yes, the city
could use a better class
of pedestrian. Your mind's
the problem. Who else
would watch the traffic cop
sauntering over & think
about foreskins smoldering
in a hospital incinerator?

PERSONAL AD 2

Handsome disabled Italian
in very fast wheelchair
wants formerly reclusive mammals
for 69, Doggie, or You On Top.
Jedi heavy-breather also
wanted, conversant with
do-it-yourself buck repellants,
able to spread blood meal,
hang mesh bags of human hair
& answer, without laughing,
the office phone: "Not Tonight
Deer. Can I help you?"

WHY I DRINK AT POETRY READINGS

Drunk on words? No,
drunk on this thermos of sangria,
my own recipe, cheap merlot,
leftover brandy, chopped-up lemons
& the tip of my right thumb
among the ice cubes, clicking,
a sound no one's noticed.
The next to last poem compares
Marxism to a bicyclist leaning
against a silver fire hydrant,
admiring his day-glo orange shoes.
I don't get it. Ask the sangria,
which I do. Consider the universe
of smells, the last poem asks us,
consider the mutt in the bookstore
sniffing the drowsy readers' legs,
his tail slapping to beat the band.
Why that cliché? That particular
dumb cliché? Ask the sangria. . . .
Me? I'm loose
as a mesh coin purse, pacific
as the slowest suicide & I
smile, clapping to beat the band.

I LIKE THE WAY IT FLOWS

The girl who
cried "Flow!"
Dyslexic. Cheerful.
No. This isn't
another "Elegy for Jane,"
his student who fell
off her horse.
"Verse" means
"turn." How should
a verse flow? How
should I know?
Call a plumber.
Lady Day sang "Love
is like a faucet, you can
turn it off & on."
But poetry? I don't
know. She didn't say.

A READING

An eland. Look, an eland! –Randall Jarrell

We're all sitting here, screwing
the caps off bottled tap water.
That's right, tap water, expressed
in plastic that leaches. Are we
stupid or what? The crème
de la crème, the postmodern,
the concerned, the anti-Amuricans.
We'd better wise up or we'll end up
writing sonnets, Italian sonnets
with only four different sounds,
pain, brain, you, few, scorch, gone.
We don't even know our even-toed
ungulates, that the common eland
& the giant eland are the same.

RECEPTION

I've been thinking about white cake
all day. Every woman I talk to
at the reception has bad breath.

You know, you try to be polite
but you just want to press a hand
over her mouth. My psychiatrist

says it's me, not them, a side effect
of the drug. What do I say
to the nice woman confiding in me,

her breath like rotting meat?
It's not you, it's me? If
wishes were horses, I'd buy

that big painting, a lustrous wall
titled "Haven," so big I'd have to
knock out my interior walls,

weight-bearing or not. Someone laughs
& says be careful what you wish for.
He'd starve if not for week-old bread
& art openings. He's here for the food.

THE NATURE OF BEAUTY

My neighbor, a physicist, tells me
he's written a monograph about
the nature of beauty. So, I ask,
what did you decide? He glares at me
like beauty's chaperone. I should wear
a bumper sticker saying no strangers,
only enemies I haven't met. Enough
about me. What about "No ideas
but in things"? How about beauty
& the variable foot? All I see is
sleepy Dr. Williams, the morning
the little girl's fever broke, looking
out the farmhouse window at, yes,
I just have to say it, the beauty
of that wet, red wheelbarrow.

LIKE

I like that expression
"the bruised earth" better
than that old chestnut
"the bruise-colored sky."
Words matter. What if
Winona's parents named her
"Barstow" or "Gallup"?
Would her ears still be famous?
Would they still dominate
the big screen like satellite dishes,
like incarnations of that song
"Little Wing"? Sometimes
I forget "pop" means "popular,"
not "short-lived" as in "poof,"
now you see it, now you don't.
Here's, like, a funny passage
from a popular novel: "I like
the clouds," somebody offers.
"They're, like, a metaphor."
"They are a metaphor," I point out.
"If they were like a metaphor,
they'd be, like, a simile." O.K.
Let's get serious now. Let's,
like, return to the bruised earth.

LECTURING MY BODY

Here's the deal: you
take care of me,
I'll take care of you.
The body's a car.
Whatever's-not-the-car,
that's the driver.
Or the car's an animal,
the driver a zookeeper.
The animal's a ditch,
the zookeeper a wheelbarrow.
A wheelbarrow bringing
tobacco, whiskey
& even love because,
well, just because.

VAMPIRISM

Red goatees? No,
dude. That's blood.

Some date —
handcuffing him to her bed,
gashing his arms,
drinking his blood.

Not one of my students
recognized the lyrics
"been a long time comin',
going to be a long
time gone." Not one.
The lore of the undead
they know. Vampirism,
the new STD. Or not.

It's shit, getting old.
I want you so much!

VEST

A pocket wobbles down the street.
Someone picks it up & takes it home.
What's more hopeful than a pocket
without a coat? I bragged I could
move in an hour, two cardboard boxes
& all my earthly goods But you get
married, have a kid or two, pretty soon
stuff owns you as the dead comedian said.
Today I walked in on my wife, naked
in the bathroom, me, not the wife, wearing
nothing but my down vest. I felt sexy,
the pillowy gray nylon hiding my bad parts.
I flexed the good parts, my guns. What's
sexier than bare arms & a sleeveless vest?
My wife laughed & said I looked gay.
That's ok. I never thought I'd be sleeping with a
60-year-old woman either.   An old Dean
of Students once told us freshmen, I can
turn my wife into a quivering blob of protoplasm
in ten seconds. I remember how we gagged.

PTEROMERHANOPHOBIA

What's the word? "Yaw"?
That's it. "To move unsteadily,
to oscillate about a vertical axis."
We're yawing, my fellow travelers & me
(fuck good grammar, I like those
"m" sounds), yawing over water
& I don't care, three valiums
& my shrink's bon voyage e-mail
good enough for me. Light turbulence,
feels like some mighty hand
playfully jiggling us in its palm
as my wife chats with her seatmate,
a bloated black guy bound for
Miami Beach & a bachelor party
somewhere, he don't know
but ain't worried. We've got
this safety net of cell phones
& taxicabs, this not-quite-shredded
mesh of concern. In the bathroom
of the hotel, still high, high, high,
I fling up my arm, knocking a diamond
off the chandelier, a pendant
which glitters among the wet towels

around my feet. My wife calls
how're you doing as I dig through
damp terry cloth & I sing out
never better, meaning I'm
yawing here, meaning I'm alive.

OTIS

The vet opens our dog's mouth
& shows us the gray mass on his palate,
the tumor that's grown so big
his breath whistles through one nostril.
Our options — $6000 for radiation
or do nothing. Goddamn anyone
who denies him a soul. My wife squats
beside him on the linoleum floor,
crooning as he whistles into her palm.

WASHING MACHINE

I give in,
bend down
& rest the side
of my head & then
my bare chest
on the lid
of the washing machine
lub-dubbing through
its rinse cycle.
Oh, heart & ear
attuned to a time-
saving appliance,
this porcelain drum
cycling moon trash,
moon trash, moon trash,
moon trash, a phrase
I'll hear for days.

MEASURING *(based on a Navajo creation tale)*

She's measuring the living room wall
where the oak shelves must go.
I like the wall bare, its swirled plaster
like low desert on which I lean my forehead
when no one's home & pretend I'm floating
over the washes. She's measuring
the bathroom door, the wicker kleenex box,
the sink where I'm naked, lathering my throat,
thinking of high desert & how First Woman
made a vagina & a penis of turquoise
& arranged them on the gray sand. She's
measuring my forearm, my index finger,
my thung & before I can press
against the porcelain, she breathes
like First Woman on my penis
& whispers to it *Start thinking.*

HELEN

She's almost 90, her forehead
like an uncloudy day. She must've
been a beautiful baby. Now
she farts during yoga, plow pose,
cow-face pose, even corpse pose,
you can hear her backfiring like
an old Vespa among the scented
candles. Nobody laughs. Certainly
not me. No jokes about gasasana,
the five inner winds, the vibrations
of the blissful sheath. I'm practicing
ujaiyi breath, pretending I'm fogging
a mirror, imagining my blurred reflection,
which is almost nothing & preparing
to bow & say the divine in me
bows to the divine in you.

ABOUT THE AUTHOR

Jefferson Carter has lived in Tucson since 1954. Currently, he is a volunteer with Sky Island Alliance. He has won a Tucson Pima Arts Council Literary Arts Fellowship, and his poems have appeared in such journals and e-zines as *Carolina Quarterly*, *CrossConnect*, *Cutthroat*, and *Barrow Street*. His chapbook *Tough Love* won the Riverstone Poetry Press Award. *Sentimental Blue*, published by Chax Press in 2007, was nominated for a Pushcart Prize. This is his eighth collection of poems.

Chax Press

Chax Press is located in the Tucson Historic Warehouse Arts
District, in the Small Planet Bakery Building. Please contact us at
chax@theriver.com, and visit our web site at *http://chax.org*, where you
will also find the chaxblog. In 2009 we celebrate our 25th birthday
with the year-long project *A Leap Is Now!* of which this book is part.
Chax Press receives support from the Tucson Pima Arts Council,
and from the Arizona Commission on the Arts, with funding from
the State of Arizona and the National Endowment for the Arts.
We depend on donations from readers like you, and you may give
to Chax Press on our web site, or contact us for more information. Here
are some of our recent titles; more are found on our web site.

Linh Dinh, *Some Kind of Cheese Orgy*
Joel Bettridge, *Presocratic Blues*
Jane Sprague, *The Port of Los Angeles*
Jonathan Rothschild, *The Last Clubhouse Eulogy*
Jacque Vaught Brogan, *ta(l)king eyes*
Jeanne Heuving, *Transducer*
John Tritica, *Sound Remains*
Patrick Pritchett, *Salt, My Love: A Ballad* (letterpress book arts)
Kathleen Fraser and Nancy Tokar Miller, *Witness* (letterpress book arts)
CA Conrad, *The Book of Frank*
Michael Cross, *In Felt Treeling*

TUCSON PIMA **ARTS** COUNCIL

Arizona Commission on the Arts

NATIONAL ENDOWMENT FOR THE ARTS